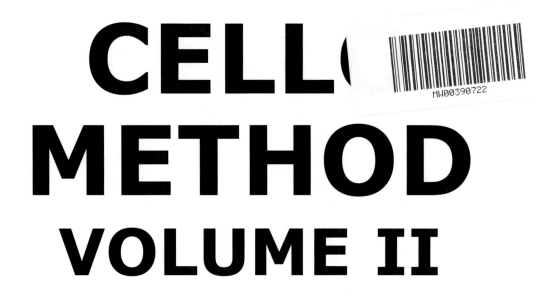

CELLO METHOD
VOLUME II

Introduction to Changing Positions

by Christine Watts

To my wonderful father
Harvey F. Watts, MD
and in his honor
to old trees everywhere

1 2 3 4 5 6 7 8 9 0

Visit us on the Web at www.melbay.com — E-mail us at email@melbay.com

TABLE OF CONTENTS

SECOND POSITION 5

   Every note in second position 7

   Sliding to every note 8

   Playing in and sliding to closed second position 9

   Second position stretch sliding to and playing in 12

   High second position 16

   Questions in second position closed 17

   Questions in second position stretched 18

THIRD POSITION 18

   Every note in third position 21

   Sliding to every note 22

   Playing in and sliding to closed third position............................23

   Third position stretch, sliding to and playing in 27

   Questions about third position closed 31

   Questions about third position stretched 32

FOURTH POSITION 33

   New notes in fourth position 34

   Every note in fourth position 35

   Sliding to every note 36

   Playing and sliding to fourth position closed 37

   Sliding to and playing in fourth position stretched 41

   Questions about fourth position closed 47

   Questions about fourth position stretched 48

EXERCISES AND ETUDES 49

YOU CAN PLAY ANY NOTE WITH ANY FINGER

Slide don't jump when you change positions.

Move your whole hand and arm at once.

Keep your thumb under your hand. Take it with you.

SECOND POSITION

Second position is one note, that is
one half step higher than first position.
To find second position, put your 1st
finger where your 2nd finger usually is.

NOTES IN SECOND POSITION

Closed position

Stretch position

High second position

High second position stretch

All notes chromatically

To get to second position, slide your first finger to where your second finger was. Make sure you move your whole hand and arm to get there, not just your first finger. Every finger moves down one note.

Every note is 1st finger

Every note is 2nd finger

Every note is 3rd finger

Every note is 4th finger

Name the notes as you play, and try to remember what finger plays each note. Pay attention to which notes are across the strings from each other.

Second position stretch. Focus on what finger plays what note.

Don't forget to maintain a good strong hand position.

Keep the pressure on your fingers when you slide to the new note. If you lift your fingers up it creates a break in the sound. We want a smooth flowing sound.

Keep your arm straight out from the side of your body and your hand up high enough so your fingers can easily stay over the notes they will play.

Even though second position is very close to first, you still need to move your whole arm and hand to the new position.

Name the note you are sliding from and the note you are sliding to. Always know what note you are playing with what finger.

Remember, even though you are only going a short distance to 2nd position, move your whole arm and hand at once, even your thumb.

Stretch your hand out as you are sliding to 2nd position, don't wait until you get there. Keep your arm straight out from the side of the cello and up high enough so your fingers can easily stay over the strings.

Press your fingers down hard and try to make them strong. Put all your fingers down at the same time as your 4th finger.

Keep your fingers close to the notes they are going to play. Arch your hand and fingers. Make them strong as they stretch.

Stay in stretch position for this whole exercise. Make sure you reach your 2nd finger all the way out to where your third finger was.

Keep your fingers over the strings and close to the notes.

Always put all of your fingers down at the same time as your 4th.

Move quickly back and forth from closed to stretched positions. Press your 1st finger down hard and do not move it.

Keep all of your fingers over the strings all the time.

Always try to strengthen your fingers. Put your fingers down hard on the strings and keep them arched.

High second position starts 1/2 step, or one note above regular 2nd position.

Closed Position

High second position stretch

SECOND POSITION CLOSED QUESTIONS

1. What note does your 1st finger play on the A string? _____

2. What note does your 4th finger play on the D string? _____

3. What note does your 2nd finger play on the G string? _____

4. What note does your 1st finger play on the C string? _____

5. What note does your 3rd finger play on the G string? _____

6. What note does your 3rd finger play on the D string? _____

7. What note does your 3rd finger play on the A string? _____

8. What note does your 3rd finger play on the C string? _____

9. What note does your 1st finger play on each string? _____

10. What note does your 2nd finger play on each string? _____

11. What note does your 4th finger play on each string? _____

12. What note does your 3rd finger play on each string? _____

SECOND POSITION STRETCH QUESTIONS

Picture your hand in stretch position on each string as you try to answer the questions. Take the time to figure out the answers if you are unsure of them.

1. What note does your 1st finger play on the A string? _____

2. What note does your 1st finger play on the D string? _____

3. What note does your 4th finger play on the G string? _____

4. What note does your 4th finger play on the C string? _____

5. What note does your 2nd finger play on the D string?_____

6. What note does your 2nd finger play on the A string? _____

7. What note does your 3rd finger play on the G string? _____

8. What note does your 2nd finger play on the C string?_____

9. What note does your 1st finger play on the C string? _____

10. What note does your 1st finger play on the G string? _____

11. What note does your 3rd finger play on the A string? _____

12. What note does your 3rd finger play on the D string? _____

THIRD POSITION

To play in third position, put your first finger where your 4th finger usually is.

NOTES IN THIRD POSITION

Start memorizing what note each finger plays on each string and what notes are across the string from each other.

Closed position

Stretch position

High third position

High third position stretch

Third position notes chromatically

Every note is 1st finger

Every note is 2nd finger

Every note is 3rd finger

Every note is 4th finger

Third position notes.

Name the notes as you play them. Try to remember which finger plays each note.

Third position stretch, reaching for a new note.

Focus on which finger plays each note.

Start with a strong arched hand and your arm straight out to the side, and keep them just right as you slide to the new position. Don't forget to keep your thumb under your second finger.

Slide slowly and carefully back and forth.

Keep your fingers close to the notes they play.

Put all your fingers down with your 4th. If you put your fingers down hard they will get stronger.

Play on your fingertips. Do not lay your fingers down on the strings. Keep your fingers and hand in a strong arch.

25

Memorize what it feels like for your left arm to make the shift from one position to another.

Always keep your fingers on the string unless you have to lift them. Reach out into stretch position as you shift.

Hold your hand and fingers in a strong arch when you are sliding from position to position as well as when you are playing. You have to work hard to make your fingers strong and well behaved so you can be a great cello player who plays music beautifully.

If you look at this exercise before you play it, you will see that you are going to slide to 3rd position stretch. Therefore, you will know that you should open your hand as you slide and not after you get there.

27

Stay in stretch position for this whole exercise. Remember to reach your 2nd finger out one note.

Keep your fingers close to the notes. Always put all of your fingers down at the same time as your 4th.

In the second measure reach your fingers out as you shift so you can land in stretch position.

Stay in stretch position.

29

When you move to stretch position, make sure you reach your 2nd finger way out and take your thumb with you, so it stays under your 2nd finger.

Keep working at memorizing and reading the notes. Relate to them across the strings also, not just up and down.

THIRD POSITION CLOSED QUESTIONS

Don't just answer these questions, spend some of your practice time memorizing the information. If you memorize the notes going up and down and going across the strings, you won't be confused when you try to find them as you play.

1. What note does your 1st finger play on the D string? _____

2. What note does your 3rd finger play on the D string? _____

3. What note does your 3rd finger play on the G string? _____

4. What note does your 3rd finger play on the C string? _____

5. What note does your 4th finger play on the D string? _____

6. What note does your 4th finger play on the A string? _____

7. What note does your 1st finger play on the C string? _____

8. What note does your 1st finger play on the G string? _____

9. What note does your 2nd finger play on the A string? _____

10. What note does your 2nd finger play on the D string? _____

11. What note does your 2nd finger play on the G string? _____

12. What note does your 2nd finger play on the C string? _____

THIRD POSITION STRETCH QUESTIONS

Pay close attention to the fact that your 2nd, 3rd and 4th fingers all play entirely new notes.

1. What note does your 2nd finger play on the A string? _____

2. What note does your 2nd finger play on the D string? _____

3. What note does your 1st finger play on the C string? _____

4. What note does your 1st finger play on the G string? _____

5. What note does your 3rd finger play on the G string? _____

6. What note does your 3rd finger play on the D string? _____

7. What note does your 4th finger play on the A string? _____

8. What note does your 4th finger play on the D string? _____

9. What note does your 4th finger play on the G string? _____

10. What note does your 4th finger play on the C string? _____

11. What note does your 3rd finger play on the A string? _____

12. What note does your 3rd finger play on the C string? _____

FOURTH POSITION

To find fourth position:

Put your thumb in the spot close to the body where the cello neck bends. Put your first finger on the fingerboard right over your thumb.

NEW NOTES IN FOURTH POSITION

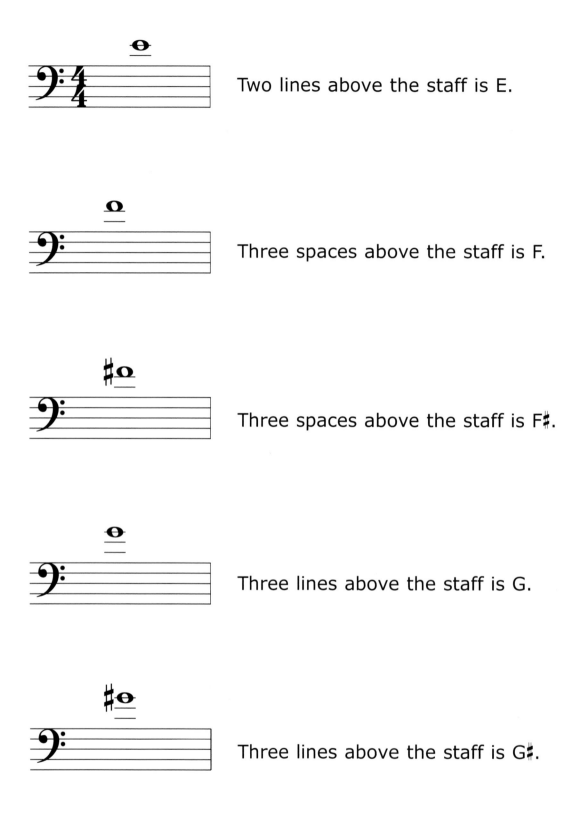

Two lines above the staff is E.

Three spaces above the staff is F.

Three spaces above the staff is F♯.

Three lines above the staff is G.

Three lines above the staff is G♯.

NOTES IN FOURTH POSITION

If your hand is in the right spot for 4th position; your 1st finger will play the same note as the string above it, except on the A string.

Closed position

Stretch position for sharps

Stretch position for flats

Every note on all strings

Make a long smooth slide which you can hear. Hold your hand up high and keep your arm straight from your knuckles to your elbow.

36

Say the note names out loud as you practice them. Go straight across the string with your fingers, but don't pull back or reach forward or you will be out of tune.

Spend time looking at the notes and visualizing where they are on the cello. Continue to memorize what notes are across from each other, and what finger plays each note.

When you make this slide, keep your arm straight out from the side of your body and move the whole thing at once with your thumb under the middle of your hand.

Stay up on your finger tips as you play, never lie your fingers down.

Put all your fingers down with your fourth. Curve them round and strong.
Listen very carefully to your notes, especially your second and third fingers.

Work for strength as well as accuracy with your fingers. Put them down hard
on the strings.

Slide carefully and slowly to the new note. Listen very carefully and check with open strings often to find out if you are in tune.

Make sure you have memorized the notes in 4th position. Memorize what finger plays what note on each string in fourth position.

Arch your fingers all the time, even when you are sliding and keep them close to the notes they play.

Stretch your hand out as you slide to 4th position so you will be ready to put your fingers down in the right places. Keep your fingers over the strings.

Remember, when you stretch for flats reach only your first finger back. Never move your other fingers, leave them in place ready to play.

When you are in 4th position the tendency is to lean your hand on the cello. Don't do that. The bottom of your hand can touch the cello, but the rest should be holding your fingers arched over the strings ready to play.

Remember to reach only your first finger back for the flatted note. Leave the rest of your fingers in place.

Put all of your fingers down with your fourth. Don't forget to reach your second finger out with your fourth.

When you reach for the fourth finger sharp, make sure you stretch your second and third fingers out also.

Always hold your left arm up high enough so your fingers can stay easily over the notes they play. Keep all your fingers over the strings all the time.

44

Remember, when you stretch for flats reach only your first fingers back. Never move your other fingers, leave them in place ready to play.

When you are in 4th position the tendency is to lean your hand on the cello. Don't do that. The bottom of your hand can touch the cello, but the rest should be holding your fingers arched over the strings ready to play.

Remember to reach only your first finger back for the flatted note. Leave the rest of your fingers in place.

Put all of your fingers down with your fourth. Don't forget to reach your second finger out with your fourth.

FOURTH POSITION QUESTIONS

Don't just answer the questions, memorize the information. Especially the notes on the A string which are new to you.

CLOSED FOURTH POSITION

1. What note does your 1st finger play on the A string? _____

2. What note does your 1st finger play on the D string? _____

3. What note does your 3rd finger play on the G string? _____

4. What note does your 3rd finger play on the C string? _____

5. What note does your 2nd finger play on the A string? _____

6. What note does your 2nd finger play on the D string? _____

7. What note does your 1st finger play on the C string? _____

8. What note does your 1st finger play on the G string? _____

9. What note does your 4th finger play on the C string? _____

10. What note does your 4th finger play on the G string? _____

11. What note does your 4th finger play on the D string? _____

12. What note does your 4th finger play on the A string? _____

FOURTH POSITION QUESTIONS

Take the time to memorize this information.

4th POSITION STRETCH

1. What note does your 1st finger play on the A string? _____

2. What note does your 1st finger play on the D string? _____

3. What note does your 2nd finger play on the G string? _____

4. What note does your 2nd finger play on the C string? _____

5. What note does your 4th finger play on the A string? _____

6. What note does your 4th finger play on the D string? _____

7. What note does your 3rd finger play on the C string? _____

8. What note does your 3rd finger play on the G string? _____

9. What note does your 1st finger play on the G string? _____

10. What note does your 1st finger play on the C string? _____

11. What note does your 2nd finger play on the A string? _____

12. What note does your 2nd finger play on the D string? _____

EXERCISES AND ETUDES

ETUDE No. 1

ETUDE No. 2

Watts

ETUDE No. 3

Matz

ETUDE No. 4

Watts

ETUDE No. 5

Matz

ETUDE No. 6

Do not lie your fingers down on the strings, stand them up and play on your finger tips. Keep your hand arched.

Matz

ETUDE No. 7

Watts

THIRD FINGER SLIDE

Watts

ETUDE No. 8

Watts

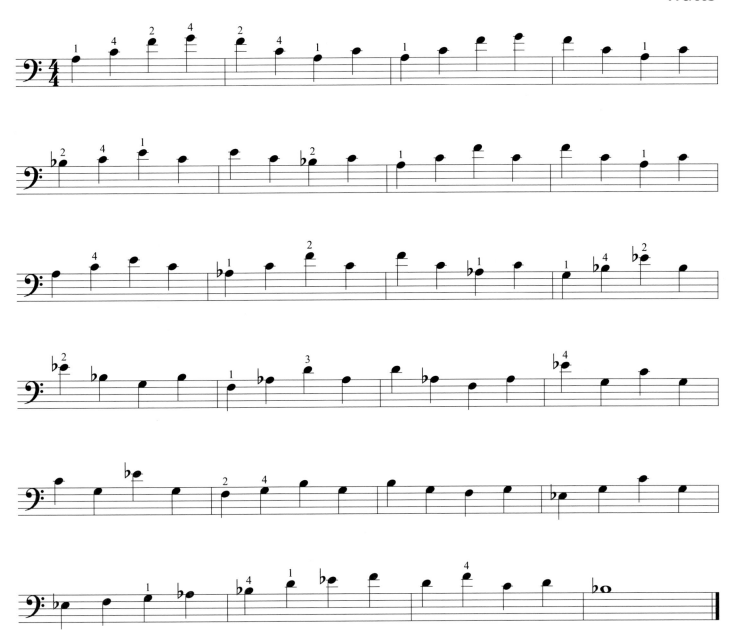

FIRST FINGER JUMP

All notes are first finger except the open strings.

Watts

Keep a good strong arched hand position.

Keep your left thumb under the middle of your hand.

Be careful, try to get the note right the first time you hit it.

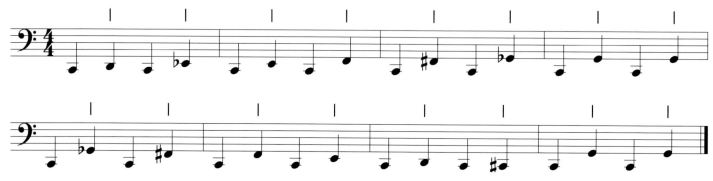

Creep slowly down each string one half step at a time.

Keep a strong arched hand position.

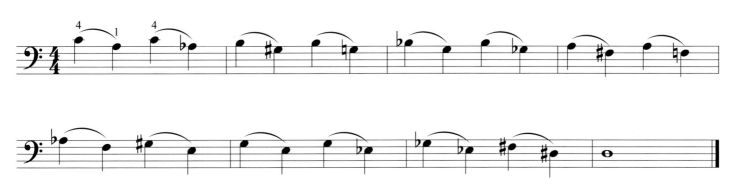

Keep your thumb under your 2nd finger.

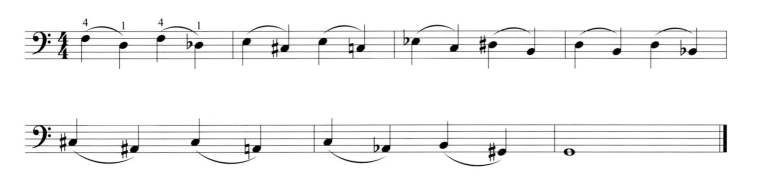

Listen carefully to stay in tune.

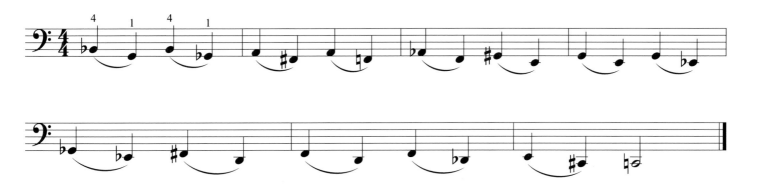

Notes

Notes